ATMOSPHERE CONDITIONS

THE NATIONAL POETRY SERIES

The National Poetry Series was established in 1978 to ensure the publication of five poetry books annually through participating publishers. Publication is funded by James Michener, The Copernicus Society of America, Edward J. Piszek, The Lannan Foundation and the Tiny Tiger Foundation.

1998 Competition Winners

Rigoberto González (New Mexico), *So Often the Pitcher Goes to Water Until It Breaks*
SELECTED BY AI
PUBLISHED BY UNIVERSITY OF ILLINOIS PRESS

Harry Humes (Pennsylvania), *Butterfly Effect*
SELECTED BY PATTIANN ROGERS
PUBLISHED BY MILKWEED EDITIONS

Joan Murray (New York), *Looking for the Parade*
SELECTED BY ROBERT BLY
PUBLISHED BY W. W. NORTON

Ed Roberson (New Jersey), *Atmosphere Conditions*
SELECTED BY NATHANIEL MACKEY
PUBLISHED BY SUN & MOON PRESS

Lee Ann Roripaugh (Ohio), *Heart Mountain*
SELECTED BY ISHMAEL REED
PUBLISHED BY VIKING PENGUIN

ATMOSPHERE CONDITIONS

Ed Roberson

NEW AMERICAN POETRY SERIES: 35

SUN & MOON PRESS

LOS ANGELES · 2000

Sun & Moon Press
A Program of The Contemporary Arts Educational Project, Inc.
a nonprofit corporation
6026 Wilshire Boulevard, Los Angeles, California 90036

This edition first published in 2000 by Sun & Moon Press
10 9 8 7 6 5 4 3 2 1
FIRST EDITION
©2000 by Ed Roberson
Biographical material ©2000 by Sun & Moon Press
All rights reserved

Cover: Todd Webb, *Sublette's Cut-Off,*
Wyoming, on the Oregon Trail, 1962
Design: Katie Messborn
Typography: Guy Bennett

LIBRARY OF CONGRESS CATALOGING IN PUBLICATION DATA
Roberson, Ed
Atmosphere Conditions
p. cm _ (New American Poetry Series: 35)
ISBN: 1-55713-392-1
I. Title. II. Series.
811'.54—dc20

Printed in the United States of America on acid-free paper.

Contents

Atmosphere Conditions

That weather when the glide path to Newark
drops the flights below gray solid slab
counties ahead of the usual time,

a lens of crotchety things that brings the lines'
logos closer for us to read, their yell
louder to our attention who don't care

to turn our aid anymore to their wolf
and fatten their audience, used to it.

That weather when you can't tell whether
what you see is yours, nature's or some curve
a public careering through throws on the wall

objects such as   Hiroshima's   shadows
or any New York subway art that glows
from that ruin or your own   ignis fatuus.

The lighting sigh of decomposition
over some settlement of the grave blows
that figure of atmosphere we named ghost,

mostly our foolishness cast by this light
against the air the rest of time is gone
from us   It burns into stone only this name

you see. Graffiti   appears only on what
is disappearing   marking the going out.

The wall the state the sainted   toppled shit on,
this signing   spray of their prefiguring star
as comet   wandered back as ghost   outlined as fallen

on the pavement sky of heaven   chalks upon
arrival   which mark defaces   which adorns,
a cloud or glory   time flies our object through.

Stars snuff out in the sun   as in the dirt
meteoric rainbow or its tornado
granted   equally hit the ground

gold pot or cash   that plasmic electric
green   they each a storm   seize each their audience
in its tracks with seeing   wish take into air

all you already have with all you want
and twisting   turn the horn's plenty to draining need

coming true.   This funnel of the light
of day   of that old blues turning at its
twenty-four and a fourth singing   "Needmore

have harm a many man…"   flattens out
to full horizon   a meteor's cards
out on the ground   It rains on your table.

Your wishes are just atmosphere   conditions
Greeks called them meteors   men made predictions
at the sight on weather   Things in the air

literally   and they believed them written
by inflammable gases   as if rainbows
and shooting stars were all a methane

as if lightning and decay venting were blasts
matter farts back at heaven,   the sight then more

a fore-spite   writing than a prophecy given,
as if that apparition of graffiti raged out
of order   of time   as of behavior.

So are   the great prophesies graffiti,
grumbles written on great weakenings   crayon
on great endings   the earth   the rainbow's crash?

What more can you see than what it is to
see   'cept the trashed meteorology
of writing on the wall   the thin air

You see the thin air before you   spell out
a holy ghost   a promise moisture of temperature,
this weather of its covenant star   this glory

in time these going out get sucked up into
but you can't really see.   a black hole

some speak of as astronomical
but you know as maybe your next breath
against air's wall of mirror   without image

which itself is a mark   a meteor
of absence
...

I. Pack

Not a real snow
in the sense that
this will be this way
only a moment
    No glacier
ever came of this
big wet fluffy
puppy feet kind
    of flakes

Almost nothing to melt
these to sloppy
tears   as also nothing
to keep the cold from packing
    into that wolf

We are straw or stick
Or we are brick
But the wolf is always.
    Trouble

The sense how
no longer pups   this makes us
her pups'
    stories we dictate

    for them to chew on   for the glacier's crib on
the ground's packed down book to turn up
for study
    out of   a watery writing this   ice on this stone

    a body
of learning to chew on

        One of the sleeping frozen
was found
on the ground outside
        one of our solid public
buildings that
        one of the daily snows
of commute
packed us in   to one by one add in
        to one of the richest

        economies on record
on the face of the earth
On the face of the sleeping frozen
        man there was not one trace of

        this

---

loss
        There were no arrows
        there was a spoon
        a knife
        No quiver   a belt
        held up

factory woven pants
scavenged technologies
for his other things
a pan
the evolved construction

of corrugated cardboard
boxes to sleep in then

He froze   This message

II. The Wanderers

The raggedy meteor homeless
  their flashing unraveling

Fortune.

Wishes nullify each other in its falling
shower.

Mine   a step in the air dissolving.

The imposed ground.   A beautiful or
It may be here   you don't want to
see something through something

else because you don't want to see it
at all when it comes down
to it   The imposed ground here   Meteors (stand for/

are a ground landing   The comet has to come around
again, torn away into   its brightness.
Gravity is in plainer language

where everything sinks in   what it stands in
for   shit   or what you call   your metaphor
or anything that refers you nearer & funky wears you apart

passing
that homeless   the sun   the words between us

she was coming towards me
through the deep erratic
lighting of the subway tunnel
the hot pinks they wore sheaths in
in the fifties in and out
of the light the shape the hips
the small waist in the dress
up close she had no shoes
her caked feet swollen she
had ground sleep leaves in her hair
as she passed my face must have
augured her open she say
sometimes
it be's that way

Could her capacity include to get loud
and yell who the fuck is this euridice
motherfucker leave my ass alone you
the crazy one punk instead of sometimes
it be's that way that either way music
doesn't do it sense doesn't the poem
turn   trying to find a surface

the ground

dream a k a augury

local or express
levels through the subway
faster   stories up through a building

to lift to the desk
transparent hours like a lunch
spent out the window: asked birds.

stories architecturalize levels
of tolerance for what so
cannot be tolerated   people die

trying
to get up
top

---

something the dealers don't conceive
of   how difficult it becomes
how difficult it is
to find a place
to live

when you often have the occasion when
you don't want to live
at all
what does this cost

when location costs when
race costs schools
cost cost costs you
your choice   what does this mean
death does   to the price & not just of real

estate

stars that wander   that fall
fire up and blow inside
out   into themselves   craters cups

that the surrounding change
falls into
     i.e.,)   step   wells   to yell
to say something in   something
else else

to find the shared
place

if there is any   there
is some
something to act as one

upon

_____

Note

1.

    the wandering star led us to planets

  and the reflectors on the bicycle's *
  wheels at night as the person of difference;

    believing geometries we've made as
  what we see we don't until we see

    the wandering star breaking the pattern
  as the pattern as none at all

---

  *

    the bicycle out of nowhere crossing the stage,
    not a trick of nature/   shuffling in disruption,
    boo boo da fool, but the hole of appearance

/

with all eight feet but singly each
upon the pedal at a time
spider anansi weaves that she's
coyote cycling.

.

.

...and she's the star.

That crater created
By your world crashing
That Clay Lady Laughing
Made into a bowl for you to beg from

That same sky

---

the very person of difference
fallen into
the hole of appearance

When I looked straight ahead
straight out ahead of the edge
of the cliff to the horizon
        The landscape as if from directly overhead
I saw down as though I had stopped
falling in that black and white which always means print.
        To my side the white wall
of the bottomless cordillera their short of the tops
hung in a hall through some length of a blizzard.
        I was black but this was the print
negative which always says
I'm not white So the mountains have shadows
        I can see through or snow
shoe A step into correction of being
lost to you who are you
        the very person of difference
falls into
the hole of appearance

III.   Laocoon on the Beach

Their term for origin   their stone
marker set to house
their start   torn down

pierced by the direction
of things in redevelopment

the old people driven by
where they used to live
point out

somewhere in a freeway
interchange

    system
      a sculpture
    of turning   twisting

threaded through   where they see
their family

wrapped in the snake
the interlaced forms   their mark
explained by the fang of the chisel left

standing a naked superstructure
What if   they had heard

the man inside the horse speared
screaming   someone
run   back into the guinea bush

refusing the sight on
those ships leapt out of the sea

IV. The Understanding

That kind of walking where
its steps are hiding places,

the witnesses not road
but ways   of turning up

that hand
that waves you through,

a trackless win.   Almost as if
not played   so innocent.

and nothing shows
up later on   a doorstep

or the line   a vanishing to
nor point.

That removal of shoe   to walk in
that retracts   the understanding.

V. Ideas of People the Builders Had

Ideas of people the builders had
still walk the spaces their failures replace

with new tries: the condos beneath the hi-rise
have overhead the cloud of halls

fallen in murder their fewer rooms
triumph over   Stupid replacement   Silent

Reasons for murder unstacked   thinned for air
like fresh plantings lined by each of the stairs

to a porch made the size of a stand to
be made   against the white wolf   the black looting

the there for the taking we're taught is ours
for just that   taking as achievement.

Others' expense part of gain   an unclear.
A design in the halls that keeps failing.

---

you pay me you
son of a bitch you pay me
i don't care what you
you just pay me i worked
for that little chump
change you pay me
you pay me

Interesting
that this song is
written on all the walls and yet
is never saved from demolition
to demolition

VI.   Bird's Blake

The located roar
        of the animals at night
                in the zoo,
the night flights
        pacing the cloud
                that forests the skies
between coasts;

where else
        safe   place
                an unseen   voiced
with the last ties whispered at dismemberment
        but where you hope
                you know what it is
by where it is.   if only word.

Star-silent footed   the planes,
        their dot prints
                lost in the trail of milky light
that winds between these horizons' walls,
        howl a point of distance   driven
                as if across an exile's blinded time

through the mark,
         your fear
                  your quickened eye at the least
movement,

so that even the sounded
         bay of bombers is less   so
                  that threatened by the world's
loosed animals
         leaves you less alone
                  and unprotected than with these
un-pinpointed crosshatches upon you
         like light,   the burglaring flash
                  the source-masking light in the dark of
something

                  outside's eye

VII. Love (of nation)
noli me tangere

Whether we were moved at the touch of the crowd
or to keep from being crushed   or at a loud
and starting gun   we are now running

everywhere we go   outracing shots state thoughts
designed deadly   intention so superior
to one   of our speeds   of our protecting skins

that it is only inattention   the limited
abilities of the aimer that saves us.

Snipers seed the loaves we run ducking to snatch;
children bounce,   extra breasts we zigzag 'cross streets
to school   swooning their gunsights exposing.

What bed in order we once had   is better tricked
pimped off and left   asleep at the gun
and our moving come   in escape through the mountains.

VIII.   Bird Population Up On Black Mountain

They warn   they say   while we're experiencing
          we can't imagine   what may be   extinctions
                    half our life away
having to hurry   to see   before something
          isn't there to see   anymore   they say
                    we don't know.   I know

a sound   almost extinct   in my life
          the new piece   of pottery   just brought home
                    from the studio   that at night
its glaze   still firing and cooling   with the house
          temperatures   the belled   ting of the glaze
                    cracking in the quiet   of the night.

To lie warm in bed   listening   beside someone
          who likes your work   and wants you to
                    bring more home   for around the house,
this   if sound tune   of my doing
          my fingers
                    stiff   is all but extinct

as if I'd dropped
            something   a clay pot   the last
                  ancestor jug flute,
carved in the base   this unknown bird
                  of my own   breath

IX. Squall

If I think of the size I was
      at certain memories,

I could see just at the level
      of the window ledge when I
recall the first time I saw
      pigeons wing-singing,

improvising their horizon
      beat by beat,   their wing
voice,   an exaltation in
      the exercising

      I see now.
If I think of the size I was
      at certain questions asked,

I think   more than I heard it said   it's called
      a squall   they are squab
        your uncles hunt them   they're (she said,
      good eating…"   And like question,

satisfying   I see now,
    getting in focus   — as commotion —
those uncertainties,   getting a bead

— within those shiftinesses of need —
on the visceral
    hunger fit of wanting to know.

Satisfying to see the felt inside
    unresolving   Patterns

almost like eating in their exactness,
    always losing the place
of any full filled with the next
    flocking movement.   Such point correcting flight,

whether in fascist peristaltic line
    or stampede randomness,
isn't the flip card that fish flash, isn't
    the fluid soap bubble iridescing

pigeon holy ghosts of color
    vanishing when they light.
Ours is the brown
    paper bag impossible to fight

our way out of
    and possible to drown
being thrown in   — stepping-stoneless —
    the crossless river.

And pigeons
        not that dove,

Theirs is the contested
    flight that hangs   or visible
possible answers on the surface
    of some internal   slugging it out
for direction
    in an invisible sack   of headlong space   that

Reminds us
    how unseen ours is   although we feel it

Feel the throwing curve a change
    of direction is,   the bottom drop out
the dive   takes and upside down the same
    weightless elation or some plan lifting off
into the lead   outdistancing
    any steps of our control

We feel punched
    back into our seats   catching up.

If I think of the size I was
made   by the excitement
    improvised on that horizon,

I see now
    the seat in an amusement   buckled in
the mind   throw me to the ceiling sky,
    side to side,   its swung argument

developing as sport   or dance
    or which least resistance
opens to escape in a riot's panic,
    its roiling perimeters   seeking like those birds'

calculations   or hosed back
    down the sky   in any case, holding
- no matter how snatched or buffeted —
    the form from within   the movement

I see now.

I stood.   I grew
        the difference in eye level
the squall of differences   of perspective
        of seeings that is

    collective,
    memory   ambiguous
    undulation

        we work like wing   within
the formation flying of our mind
        that flock of / in
time

X.   If You Think of the Size

If you think of the size
         you were
                  at certain memories,
you would
         hold yourself
                  without thinking
now on your lap
         is how you thought
                  you'd watch   from the tops of trees
what grown up
         sight sees,

hold like a child how
         trains side by side
                  floated underground
in different rooms seen
         through the different window speed
                  being small
in some one's arms is
         If you think of the change.
                  How it all
side by side floats
         in some ground

on a subway yesterday or years ago
        on a night
                train south.
How you'll understand
        as an undergrad the
                popular relativity
explanation model
        from that kid
                kinetic parallax memory
education some mystic escape trick   to stay ahead of
        Move that nigger baby

so's I can sit there or
        I'll get the conductor.
                And not being moved.
Passed years ahead
        through Montgomery-parted waters
                and those children's Birmingham
learning   I
        Shall not
                I shall not be moved
and not being moved
        not moved.

.....

The wonder of the movement
        was the feeling
                of being right
of being understood
        As being
                Right
The unity of that
        probably the only
                time we felt
at one
        with this country
                felt to belong
felt not to be opposed
        put out   put down
                put off
we were not outside
        there was no war
                in that warring
moment we
        were in that land and
                in that land the "We
all is one" were free   that land the
        Freedom
                we all prayed about

This is a common feeling:
    a commonweal
      we feel
          lost.

XI.   When Change

When change
    came the terror
        they thought
it would hit
    and be over
        with
the worst

a waited out
acclimation;

they never
    thought simply
        change
would change
    into change and
        the always
be

that instead of
something.

*

*

It isn't a railroad train
    in an outburst
drumming the tracks
    getting on up

from here   to there
    changing spots   out of
restlessness tonight
    it is the wind

I hear through
    the chimney
 as through any
    open

    window horn
put to my ear.

The sea
    has always had
its peace
    through shell to say

how much
       each wave ending
a zero more
       it can't sit still

The hearth's conch
       its breath curling
an echo of the steam
       engine boogie drumming

       of train track blues
is really attuned   of the heart.

              *

*

that track)
That beating   has never been cut down

Not through forced relaxation
     of law   nor the deep breaths surfacing
the ghettoes gave   nor the opening
     into stations the body works

That body which by
     having no weight
kept the heart
     rate high

has never been cut down
     swings
at the slightest sound
     into movement

into voice

I hear the have to
    keep moving in the same
ability I have to   see
    Can't see the air for

it telling me   move —
    like one by one the trees ditty
bop a breeze down the block
    — my black ass   but

No longer out of anyone's way
    The way has changed to my way
So I am with it   But I can always
    Tell the wind risin'   leaves

    tremblin' on the trees tremblin'
on the trees

48

XII.   Afognak

There are islands   volcanoes
have covered with a light
dust   inches deep

that years   later
the layer shutting off the light
and air from the water life

in the lakes   settles
filters   cleans like an
alchemical fire   purifies

the element water to
a point so abstract a perfect that
the natural   lake is sterilized

There are flora   whose skins
a fallout surfaces with dark
the light   dust closes off

that night   buries
worm-cast above the ground
'til empty inside   a famine's

sculpture mold   (its live
fit lost)   of disappearance
into landscape   ghosts the landscape's flower

a moss topiary
of once stones and barely growth
covered niggers of the burned trees

There are fauna   the humans
themselves one have fit
themselves into   systems

ideas   as niches
that give out   like races   churches
colorations of nations'

flags   mummifications
(wch if anyone's left to)   unfurl
dissolve   into that pool of mirror

thin air is   that yet
flies the blackening sun
that standard   of clarity

XIII.   Whatever

Whatever formlessness
a lizard moves like in the dark   stripped
out of lit shape as out of that
suited sight he changes against   tonight

slits through the woven reed transom
above the windows everyone has told me
to sleep with shuttered
against snakes.   Windows

the eyes of course.   And the transom
opening in the forehead above them
for breathing through   dream   and for —
Air itself   a lizard comes through the hair.

And, mammal,   in the river sweat of these dreams
I float asleep naked on my back.

River porpoises have human forms
so incredibly beautiful they drop
— as if dead at that beauty — enraptured mates to the ground
who feel it heaven's.

One woman had an orgasm ten days;
a man ejaculated for one week.
He lives naked preaching from the shallows now
how the porpoise's feather headdress hides their nose

hole,   urging everyone in.
We have these contacts all the time with
metamorphosis   Whatever
window what opening what eye out on

the changling site   the sighting shows our difference,
that what we cover doesn't hide nor change us.

Babies' peekaboos   the papal leaf as if
underwear doesn't come off   more sexy
pretending the unseen   that what we cover
doesn't hide nor change us so much as

make us the assignment of witness
make it so we're not here but for seeing,
and our only changes   :of integrity,   of
how undivided our self returns

from masking from disguise from changing side
from all the saving disloyalties   uneaten,
to be seen complete,
the stature with the balls and penis on.

Lizard comes to show its growings back one who,
when best, has a gift for change that leaves change intact.

XIV.   Dance Guede Name

All my dances lean against falling
Not partners   All my dances
are done proud but step

falling   All my dances have
their arms down with
no one to be around so

all my dances never uplift
their arms
around the neck of falling to crown it faith

their fingers
around the neck of falling
let faith go given

what faith gives
All my dances lean dangerously
Alone & Against

It.   I was told
it was bad luck
to sit in a chair reared back
balanced on two legs   No one said

Guede
did this that this

was an African memory
of the god of affront who
vexes gravities
sitting like this   balanced between

this world and the next
still on two feet

I just thought it was sexy
but that is he   that he   guede too
All the people you see running away
know how he loves

to dance   All my dances
lean against falling

Not partners   All my dances
take the name
pride but the step
falling

XV.   Phat Ptah, Nawlins

the blat trombone
  tonguey sound

                    small
          propeller aircraft

make like
  children trying to

      be irritating
off the wall

    you can't tell which
        direction they're coming from

and have to look up

    which is part what
        they are part what they want

which is that rude   again
   blat at your face fun
      part of being

up there
   in the sky   in
      that image

XVI. Told What No One Has Seen in Ibolo

Two dead people carry a log
    slit drum rotted with sacrifice
        caked blood
The instant you see it hear you
    hear it
        you can't hear it anymore

The dancers shaken
    like rattles
        flesh beaded bone   gourds
are   at first you thought
    singing
        are trying to catch   their breaths
shrieking away from them
    down the road
        the road that is singing
up in terror a shield of dust
    between its way
        and their feet

They are mad
    boys they say
        whose backs are broken by
the can't be of their steps
    but are dancing
        now   not people.
They couldn't be
    Because they precede
        something even further
not
    here

Bury all the house fires under water
    or inside the stomping foot
        stone   in the floor
Any lights in the house
    tape down
        with darkness

Bury all of outside under
    the dirt when this
        happens that
shutters are
    Say goodbye
        Everything outside is lost

until this passes
    Even some of
        that after
won't be left
    No one wants to know

what this mask is:
    Though we all know she did,
        Mama Ti died without ever saying
she saw it as a child.   We know
    Papa Nukku grabbed her
        from her peeping through the gate
and ran and hid in the bush for one moon.

When the eldest nephew died an old man,
    the secret chiefs chased everyone
        out of his house
They dug up the floors
    There was something burning
        inside the house for four days.
When they left   everyone knew
    we were always afraid
        it would come   but it had been here
all along under our feet.

XVII. ... Making Ground

The sun throws its shadows down behind things
in honor   In some daze, under another
cast, my heart forgets   the float suspends
time   waiting falls in all its one directions
— a case my foot forgets is possible.

Legba lays out all the forks before me
around me   The road, shadows behind things,
— a cast my case forgets is possible —
is a full circle of glory   rainbow's ring
that Legba say in his case honors we.

We have this choice   — which throws a light on us —
of things to try a way through by attention,
who have only the darkness of not knowing
within to offer   to throw beneath the feet

...Making ground.

XVIII.   Down Break Drum

How a fish might
        look up and
    see the still stalker
            heron,

in the West Indian Day
        Parade crowd
    I turn at the
            stilt walker's loud

grand baton foot
        clearing
    a silence
            swept smooth of scared

people backed before
        the bow wave
    its step
            in their noise wakes.

And I am the one
        caught.
    This is what folks talk
            about the gods walking

sitting on your shoulders
in your shoes
having consumed
you

in that beauty

fixed by
that crack of the gavel

your decision made

to face and see.

XIX.   I Don't See

I expected something up out of the water
not the shadow in the wave that rose

to fill the wave then splash a breath
off the abutting air   then disappear.

I didn't see any of this   only
the dark waves.   Even the size of a whale

I don't see   what I look directly at.
I didn't see the pronghorn antelope,

speed they pointed out equal our car's;
but never having seen distance so large

I couldn't pin in it   point to antler,
and saw in parallax instead   the world

entire a still brown arc of leap   so like
a first look at the milky way   each stone

a star I saw but could not see.
I didn't see

the Nazca earth drawings looking at a line
like a path   the vision on it   my not looking up.

& trying to see from on the ground looking
from a plane thousands of feet above,

maybe I saw only what the unenlightened
marking out the lines could see from there

because I never saw the figures
until shown from books.

I've told folk half the truth   that I was there I was
but embarrassed   never told   I missed my chance

until I saw: without embarrassment
this country miss its chance   looking at color

and not see what it looked directly at,
without embarrassment

act   and not see that done
on its own hands   not see its own bright blood.

XX.   I Remember Form

I remember a yellowish color
       suddenly opening in the ground
       just to my left a step ahead
       when I startled a huge adder
I remember the sound it beat
       with its tail in the leaves
I remember the only thing I actually saw
       clearly was the tail withdrawing
       into the muck of the leaves on the jungle floor.

I remember the red brown skin of the porter's
       legs slipping in the mud climbing up
       into the shadows of the overgrowth
       hanging into the deep bed of the stream
I remember the flash of
       red and the machete at the same time
       coming down right behind the heel
       of his own foot and taking off the head
       of the one snake we'd carried
       the antidote against   knowing it is useless

I remember months after being home
       taking off my shirt and pants
       hanging the belt across
       the seat of the chair and the weight of the buckle
       slowly sliding the brown leather down to the floor
I remember jumping naked
       halfway across the room
I remember I did this
       again
       as recent as two weeks ago

The Osiris Addendum

I remember the shock
       of remembering
       that I am
still that   who
       rememberings
       re-member

XXI. Monad

In the same construct by which
    he can't see behind himself
        he can't see what haunts,
what weighs on him   in
    a way that
        makes him hunted
horizon to horizon.
    So behind that,
        everything he can't see

becomes round as around him,
    and he can feel it behind
        one of those grains of sand
out there,
    their size,
        but that weight,
like the change in
    the density of his penis   at night
        when he's asleep,

the huge limbed picasso
    and botero women in art,
        or balloons
dim and small as smog
    particles dance whole
        atmospheres up to him

a vast complete and piercing
    weighing of his want
        and sky

against the crumb of his blood

XXII.   Strata

She lay in the bottom of the boat
        he rode
the boat she lay in the bottom
        of the top of the lake
the lake she lay in the bottoms
        of the lay of the land
the land lies like a crust they say
        on the jelly of the earth
        as on her thighs he does
            dried stuff

        turned to sugar

like light turns to crystal when the water
        moves she
moves it moves he   the
        bio   geo
sphere's layers cocked   open estruate   warp
        by water or by heat
peel back   naked from each
        lamina of clothes come loose
        as all love is: the seeker.
            its met: the questioner as honest

    in the answer as in the getting of.

the line   like arm the gunnel one
        side at a time's move
reaches up around the level's
        bubble on his back as
the plumb line   takes over fucking balanced
        in the rocking
wave   load by load dissolved back
        into sea the earth the table
        water sweetening
           a well

      she lay in

She lay in the bed the buried
        city he lay desert over
her
        sanding away that she
lay in the bottom of
        the boat he lay in
the hold of
        the ship their cross was
        In
           In one piece made

their Sun.
       ol hannah's osiris
       and what rivers
       and mississippis mean to us

he lay in   the hold of
        that ship
their held   she lay in the hold
        of
their sun drawing a hand   of water
        that would keep
the grass sea deep and unthirsted
        us
        in what   we float
            but cannot drink

       this crystal bubble

this bottle message of
        our salt darkness
        a sea a glory a

       fully sphered sky!

XXIII.   Through Which You Cross Over

How is it like that
   city
        itself:
the driving into manhattan

   is rafted instead
      under the river
leaving dry
   the memory of any

      washing away
we prayed for   got here?

of even the connection
   of water to   as if
     the neckbone were not
connect to   and his face balloons,

   made worlds,
     made way   to no sense except as
mapping's blowing wind-cheeked totem making it
   on in   making land fall as music,

        the cadillac swung on
(dishistorical horn.

& Whose horn
    (rephrased as whose death
          as whose absence we've
just gone through   got here

    like that city   suddenly   Dizz
        's music   appears around us
charted in the as it is as if
    we are here again forever the music

    on before
we even get here   got here

        ... *for/*   *to carry me home*   swinging our
        sense of the eternities

XXIV.   Broadway Boogie-Woogie

yellow squares and rectangles
s'posedly new york taxis

in a grid of streets seen
from a roof but flat on

the painting and all
the cabbies' languages

nowhere near that orderly
or near as

a street we really knew by
playin' off

the form and these musicians
dizzy in there with them

piled in the back
rappin' 'bout this painting

someone seen and someone says

say dizz hey who was dutch
hey dizz say was who dutch
hey dizz dizzy
                    played through
you know if you
couldn't play wouldn't
nobody understand you

dizz you talkin'
'bout the painting

right?
right

XXV. Blues: In The Face Of

...condescending
        notions of immediatist,
            nonreflective blackness."

Without a case nothing   on my face
        I go to pieces   I can't see
                myself clear
Without moving a muscle
        I break   down and cry
                without a tear

It's often said to be
        unexplained   why
                black men have
this behavior
        or if they have
                any at all

in response to
        the face they see
                their own
face make
        on faces
                they routinely see

the feelings there
        their share
                But whose tears

:

my interiority
think of it
as a bit of Ellington take-home
in an elegant
silver case

dropped on entering
the curved chrome
the onyx glass and windows
of skyline lights
type

of place but since
it's home
now   a little greasy
soft
too leftover to heat,

room
or is it
body   temperature,
a single
body

XXVI.   I Am in Blue (or The Changes)

Done this so often   the days
have worn the date off
the doing   the number
slash number slash number
in the upper right hand corner

as empty of any sense to me
as the state's form code
lower left   usually
near a box where I
name   title)   work

which *must* be in blue pen
like all changes,
deletions in red,
questions in pencil.
This is in pencil.   I will change

it into print   if it's not lost
somewhere in all this

that same in the designation
same ol' same ol'
is that named
in Langston Hughes' *Same
In Blues*   it seems to me

this nullification in the same
-ness of the unrelieved is
the blues he's talkin' about
blue in even the navajo sense blue being
nonexistent not even the color black

so life and the blues both
amount to just about nothing and the changes
having to be in blue
pen in these justification rosters
countin everbody like theys niggahs

is some heavy hues I'm doin'   hey
                rebop de bebop   bam type shit
        you won't hear at bam   in brooklyn jim
                    ok? ok,   back to work
                    Done this   so often

XXVII.   Cornerstone

(for Jake Milliones

Brick has had this wait before
    how long before
        it's torn
down carrying
    nothing

        weighing in
a coliseum
    grounding out a service
        road   a cobble street
the crushed floor

    the borrowed of the poor
        not our
new idea of environ
    -ment   the other
        continuous

meant by the gleaners'
    beggared pick up
        of the field:
the housing stock
    just sitting

        in the cities   brick and board

droppings of famine
    undigesting bone and
      useless wrapping
the liquid bright
   copper

     ripped out for market.

    *

*

The
copper placed on the scale dish
    to be weighed judged to be worth
        so much baby need
a new pair shoes
    the heart placed
        in the prone Aztec stone man
dish balanced on his stomach
    We place our heart
        on   our poverty
such as god / we
    are nothing
        and it don't mean a thing
the scale still
    motionless
        we are paid.

The collectors
    bag people   hunter-gatherers
        the connoisseurs
yellow leaves or none or few as frame
    -like time
        conspire to put things up.

Or
someone come along & see
    he / maybe / the   one fragment
        pick it up
put it in place
    a musician an unsocial
        social architect or

someone tall all legs
    no neck and little
        bad feet
put up a house
    again people can get in
        get off their dogs
& on they own
    We

        have had this wait
before
    (for
        Jake

      *

*

There is that shiver
    up the spine we get we say
        is someone walking on our grave

There is the sense
    we quote of standing on the shoulders
        of giants as though rote

we step only the upward
    But it is in our hands to lay
        what is under our feet

& what makes the distinction
    between being
        walked on and being stood upon

when we see the city
    walking around in his
        works walking in what we have

of now
    if not the golden streets
        Brick

has had this wait before.
    (This is for
        Jake

XXVIII.   Call From Vandall

(for Dick Vandall

The machinery of the air, the works
that never jabs up into the perceptions,
was caught out of some corner of the ear
floating barely above his subliminal,
unmoving   so unlike song.
He'd contacted his senses   or picked up
his perception before fully leaving
one state and so experienced his own

arrival in another   his eyes opening
and he was crying.
He often cried in his sleep thereafter.

The crying seems only a part of
something he was doing from the same
but larger place, a voice larger than voice is
here,   a heart deeper than one could stand for
in one body and not be lost as   yet.
Yet he awoke   wet with it   on his face
and the sense that nothing happened
in the last to preclude its being in
this present.   Only

in different character he feels the same.
The same beings lost, left or killed
people this, people here with some vague sense
of some history   of passage together
before   through this   as if a room
their mother walked through before each arrived.

Then he felt so many he forgot
and picked up where he was.

                              The huge house...
              The many mansions
A bell ringing in the empty sky

XXIX.   untitled / unfinished

                    dry has got
the moth wing soot sky
                    of its universe
                              on his fingertips
to gaze in-

                    to   he got
touched picking up the
                    flutter of the heat
                              his name   crazy as
a yellow

                    sand lizard's
trail spelling   reads like
                    an error figures
                              in his fingerprints
wave him off

                    from landing
on   his name is drawn
                    on a heat   and his:
                              blood   homed in on the
heart's press

                    lays him in
its way   the drawings
                    pulled from his fingers'
                              touch touch   laminate
of one stuff

XXX.   I Know Jack

A dazzle of late afternoon
sun overwrites the edge of the building

It's gone   because too much
cannot be read into a subject if light pours out

All this displacement's apartments remain for later
return and all clear   however silent

A celebration   that pick up where you left
to return with more   meaning what

That blindness pulled over on you
restores your sight

But the sight is never all clear nor the sound
voicing so   showing outside the lines

The polymaths of obliteration erase the board
Faster than the board is

Poetry even faster is
All over

XXXI.   The Dark One's Appearance

An attic split in two by a stairwell—
the rail intimidated to invisible
at the hole— in what little light
the bright end windows brought to the center—

He sat on a trunk backed to that edge—
one leg in half lotus the other hung
his foot not touching down — he floated up
ash gray over the trunk's black ground—   his skin

the house burned down color—   his shining hair
like wrinkled waves of wood carbon   char
silvered at the highlights of its black—
the same black   his eyes   the clear whites showing

recognized me   knowing I would come—
old unmet friends finally here— to face
a high window open above the solving
ground   distance no matter   the passage found

Then there an ancient mother on the steps—
only her head— her argument we've had
before— I turn to and when I turn again
to him he's gone the brilliant window

empty and without me— he has either
jumped or flown— I have no way of knowing

XXXII.   Afraid of Fire I Don't See

Afraid of fire   because I haven't seen
fire   as in both seen and been in
and have only foreseen

the barren homelessness after
in the ashes   I seem to know
what to do in the ashes   where I come in

even in my dreams   the long log of that entrance
almost as the nature of this world
and living   is as if in aftermath

of dangerously conflagrant lives
which the small inner fires of our marches
meant to be a break to   be their containment.

And afraid of what I could set
and walk away from without seeing

I see the cold cross as gold and not the fire
burning   on either lawn nor bush   but torched ledgers
the constant outbreak of (and   grieved unsettlement

 fires which our prosperities set in others'
greed that jealously burned down our proofs
of towns as black worlds   I dream of

behind me   My eyes opening   moving on
and in this waking reading in these faces
what I dreamed   in the unwash of ash

we have   as a family for skin.
Afraid of fire because I carry on
this face because of fire   an energy of ash

to rise again   and again afraid of what I have set
and walk away from without seeing

XXXIII.   Sight

Deep pack white snow
black moonless night

the black spars of the burned house
the roof gone

Up the top of the stair   still glowing
the one holding nail

one star in the sky
distant, indifferent   center

XXXIV.   Disengage

The mapwork
    tangle of hoses
        disengages
The withdrawal   a growing over
    of the failure to get there by
        now what is here:
Someplace awkward
    in its in-
        habitability

Figures stepping over   now
    Merely historical supply
        Lines   of necessity

packing up
    saying in the dark
        as if
to Zimbabwe
    Chichen Itza   our lives
        are now
Someplace else
    ...

     ...

Look at the one waving
    feathery top branch
        on the outline of trees
as flown
    should you   also moving
        turn to look back
and gone
    extinct   one of you
        among many connections

XXXV. Archaic Song FM

The turning of whatever
          spinning instrument
her time used turned her
          minutes into death

And she would be wound in this
          as in earth
          when her long breath
around the sun completes its skein

and from this fuse
          a fabric of which
mother of silence pieces this
          explosion of starry "O

          I cannot finish" and
"O will it come-o
…. My love,
          the metro moves along

a dial   station to station
          None of the faces finishes
its song
          in that window

All of the spinning songs
        we know of
        have no end
The stringy girls thicken into cord

helixing into some next else's
        turn   turning in the beds
themselves instrument
        playing

        out the lines
that knotted   clothe the singing

...

the shooting star/
the falling star
the wish
the crashing meteor
the crater
the bowl for you to beg from
    this
answer

NEW AMERICAN POETRY SERIES (NAP)

30. *New and Selected Poems,* Charles North
31. *Polyverse,* Lee Ann Brown
[WINNER NEW AMERICAN POETRY SERIES COMPETITION 1996]
33. *The Little Door Slides Back,* Jeff Clark
[WINNER NATIONAL POETRY SERIES 1996]
34. *Tales of Murasaki and Other Poems,* Martine Bellen
[WINNER NATIONAL POETRY SERIES 1997]
35. *Atmosphere Conditions,* Ed Roberson
[WINNER NATIONAL POETRY SERIES 1998]

For a complete list of our poetry publications

write us at Sun & Moon Press
6026 Wilshire Boulevard
Los Angeles, California 90036

SUN & MOON PUBLICATIONS OF THE NATIONAL POETRY SERIES

1994 / Pam Rehm *To Give It Up*
[selected by Barbara Guest]
1995 / Julia Spahr *Response*
[selected by Lyn Hejinian]
1996 / Jeff Clark *The Little Door Slides Back*
[selected by Ray DiPalma]
1997 / Martine Bellen *Tales of Murasaki and Other Poems*
[selected by Rosmarie Waldrop]
1998 / Ed Roberson *Atmosphere Conditions*
[selected by Nathaniel Mackey]
1999 / Standard Schaefer *Nova*
[selected by Nick Piombino]